Little Rudy Rooster
and Granny's Fried Bread

Written and Illustrated by:
Jeanie M. Smallwood

proving press

Book Design & Production: Columbus Publishing Lab
www.ColumbusPublishingLab.com

Copyright © 2025 by Jeanie Smallwood
LCCN: 2025920891

All rights reserved. This book, or parts thereof, may not
be reproduced in any form without permission.

Paperback ISBN: 978-1-63337-974-9

Printed in the United States of America
1 3 5 7 9 10 8 6 4 2

Dedication

This book is in honor of Granny, Arietta Fisk Stull.

Granny was the mother of nine. When her children were young, they didn't have electricity or running water. They would haul water in buckets a quarter of a mile.

It was a bumpy, uneven walk, and many times my dad's bucket was only half full by the time they arrived home. Yet many of the people from town who had running water and electricity would come to Grandpa and Granny's to eat on Sundays.

That tradition lived on in her family. When I was young she lived in a very tiny house, and on Sundays the family would all pile in for dinner.

She was known as Granny to everyone she knew. She was famous for her Johnny Cakes (fried bread).

Every year the community center in her hometown of Port Washington, Ohio, holds a fundraiser called Granny Stull's Johnny Cakes Day. Family and friends come to enjoy Granny's recipe. (Her Grandson Terry has kept her Johnny Cake tradition alive, making them at his church and the fundraiser.) This is only fitting since Granny was very community oriented. She was very active in her church, The First Baptist Church, which is now the community center.

She made the most delicious and beautiful cakes. She crocheted gifts for her family and friends. Once, she and her daughter-in-law Linda crocheted vest for the basketball team. The team wore them during warm-ups.

Granny was one special lady with a generous, giving heart, and the work of her hands made an impact on her community that will be forever remembered.

Once upon a time
there was a little rooster named Rudy...

He woke up early one morning
and went to see his dad at the barn.

Along came Polly Pig all pleasingly plump. She yelled, "Who wants to make mud pies down by the dump?"

"Oh, not I," said Rudy Rooster.
"It's such a beautiful morn,
and I'm helping my dad plant some corn."

Polly Pig rolled her eyes and went on her way, thinking, *All that work makes for a boring day.*

Along came Darren Duck
all proper and prim.
He said, "Hey, Rudy Rooster,
want to go for a swim?"

"Oh, not I," said Rudy Rooster.
"The day is growing hotter.
I'm helping my dad, the corn to water."

Darren Duck rolled his eyes and went on his way, thinking, *All that work makes for a boring day.*

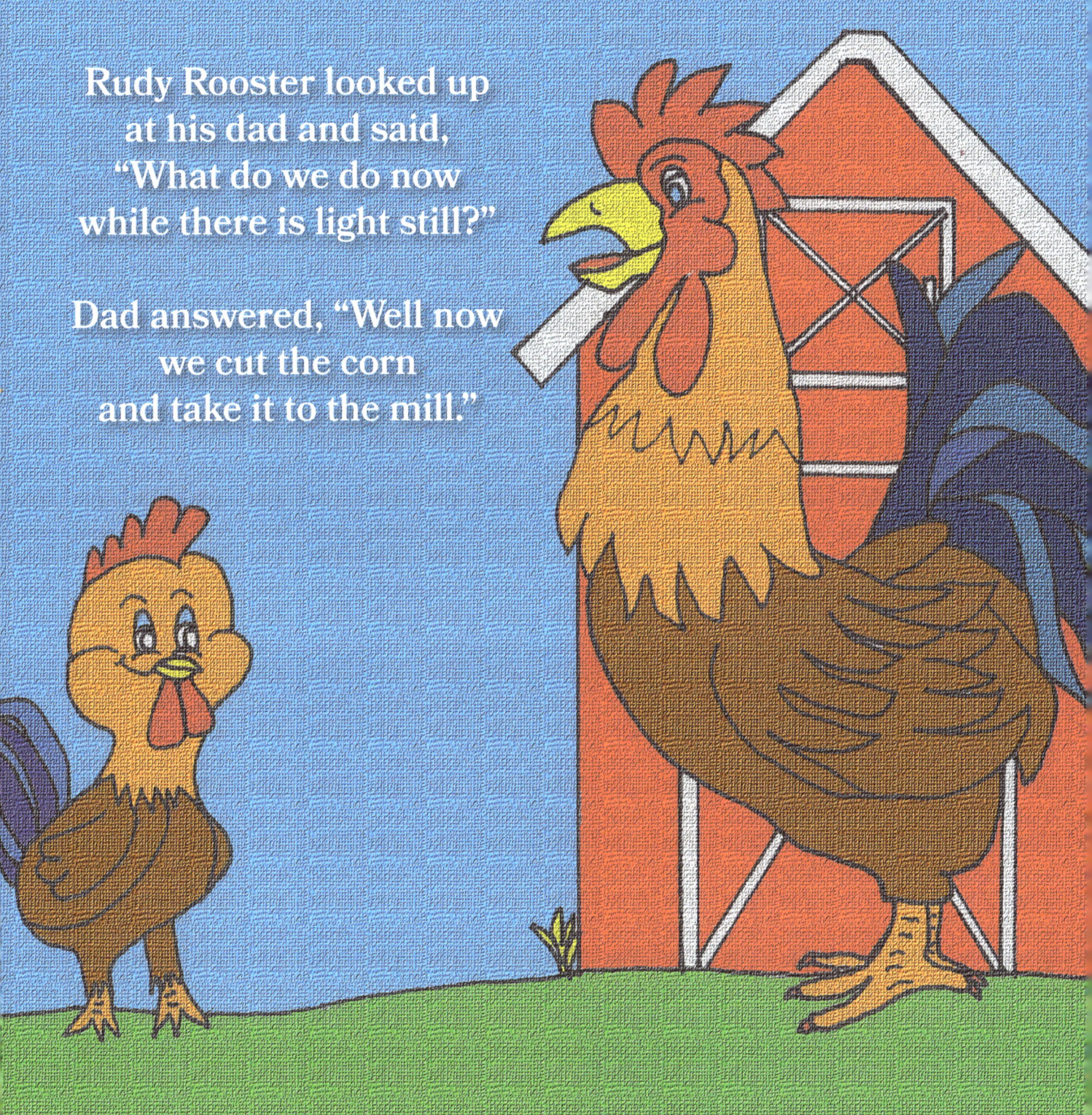

Along came Callie Cat full of sass and charm.
She yelled, "Hey, Rudy Rooster!
Want to chase mice in the barn?"

"Oh, not I," said Rudy Rooster. "That sounds like a thrill, but I'm helping my dad take the corn to the mill."

Callie Cat rolled her eyes and went on her way, thinking,
All that work makes for a boring day.

Rudy's momma said,
"Oh how blessed we are
to have all this corn.
I will make something
special with it
in the morn."

Morning came,
Rudy Rooster woke up early and
jumped up wide awake.

He said, "What are you making, Momma?"

She said, "I'm making some cake."

"Can I help you, Momma? What does it take?"

As Rudy's family sat down to eat,
the aroma of the corn cake filled the street.

"What is that?" everyone asked.
"What a delicious smell."
But where it came from,
nobody could tell.

Along came Haley Horse, prancing down the street.
She yelled, "Hey, Rudy Rooster!
Want to grab a bite to eat?"

"Oh, not I," said Rudy Rooster.
"Your invite is very sweet,
but I'm helping my dad plant some wheat."

Once the wheat was all ground,
they took it home safe and sound.

Granny was there and said,
"Oh what a blessing
to have all this wheat.
In the morning
I will make a
special treat."

Morning came,
Rudy Rooster woke up early,
and jumped out of bed.

He said, "What are you
making, Granny?"

She said,
"I'm making fried bread."

"Oh I love your
Johnny Cakes!
Can I help?
That sounds fun,
you know."

Along came Timmy Turtle ever so slow.
He yelled, "Hey, Rudy! Let's race.
How fast can you go?"

"Oh, not I," said Rudy Rooster.
"Maybe tomorrow, though.
Today I'm helping my granny
knead some dough."

The next day, the animals gathered to hear
what Lionel the Lamb had to share.

As always,
everyone was there.

The farmer wasn't home, and word started to spread.
They were all hungry, and wanted to be fed.

The chicks came to Lionel Lamb
all in a flutter.

"What should we do?
Everyone is starting to mutter."

Lionel Lamb said, "No need to worry.
Do not despair. You give them something.
What do you have to share?"

Lionel Lamb said, "Bring it to me and have everyone sit down."

Lamb blessed the food
and had the chicks pass it around.

They began to ask Rudy,
"Where did this bread come from?
It is quite delicious!"

He said, "Haven't you noticed?
I've been about my father's business.
One thing he's taught me and one thing I know,
is that in life you reap what you sow."

The animals ate
until they had their fill.
And when they counted,
there were twelve baskets still.

Although this story has come to an end,
and this story is just pretend.

There is a real story about a
boy with some fish and some bread.
He gave it to Jesus
and five thousand were fed.

If you want to hear the real story
about the boy who was willing to share,
look in the Bible you'll find it there.
John 6:1-14

About the Author

Jeanie Smallwood loves to write children's stories about the friendship, love, and kindness of God.

With colorful illustrations and heartfelt characters, Jeanie aims to inspire readers to be confident, brave, loving, kind, to do good, be generous, be ready to share, and to know how special they are.

Jeanie lives in Ohio with her husband. She treasures time with her family, prayer, worship, sharing the word of God, and enjoys writing Christian devotions and poetry.

www.ingramcontent.com/pod-product-compliance
Lightning Source LLC
LaVergne TN
LVHW070949070426
835507LV00030B/3469